FIRST, FOURTH *and* LAST

JONATHAN LUCAS Ph.D

Order this book online at www.trafford.com/06-2890
or email orders@trafford.com

Most Trafford titles are also available at major online book retailers.

© Copyright 2007 Jonathan Lucas.
All rights reserved. No part of this publication may be reproduced, stored in a retrieval system, or transmitted, in any form or by any means, electronic, mechanical, photocopying, recording, or otherwise, without the written prior permission of the author.

Note for Librarians: A cataloguing record for this book is available from Library and Archives Canada at www.collectionscanada.ca/amicus/index-e.html

Printed in Victoria, BC, Canada.

ISBN: 978-1-4251-1131-1

We at Trafford believe that it is the responsibility of us all, as both individuals and corporations, to make choices that are environmentally and socially sound. You, in turn, are supporting this responsible conduct each time you purchase a Trafford book, or make use of our publishing services. To find out how you are helping, please visit www.trafford.com/responsiblepublishing.html

Our mission is to efficiently provide the world's finest, most comprehensive book publishing service, enabling every author to experience success. To find out how to publish your book, your way, and have it available worldwide, visit us online at www.trafford.com/10510

 www.trafford.com

North America & international
toll-free: 1 888 232 4444 (USA & Canada)
phone: 250 383 6864 ♦ fax: 250 383 6804 ♦ email: info@trafford.com

The United Kingdom & Europe
phone: +44 (0)1865 722 113 ♦ local rate: 0845 230 9601
facsimile: +44 (0)1865 722 868 ♦ email: info.uk@trafford.com

10 9 8 7 6 5 4 3 2

Introduction

June 6, 1971 was a Sunday. I remember many details of that day and there are probably many that I do not. Of course, the details quickly recalled are most vivid and heartwarming. To extract the other details, which are a little deeper in the recesses of my mind, requires some research. Research is what I do for a living. I am a research psychologist by training. My father unloaded trucks and later worked as a sandhog with one of his brothers and my older brother. My mother worked many years for the New York Board of Education as a paraprofessional and a school secretary. My parents instilled in me respect for education and hard work. As native New Yorkers, they also instilled in me a love and appreciation of the Yankee tradition.

I am sure I went to Mass that day at St. Stanislaus Church on the Lower East Side of Manhattan. As I left our apartment, I said good-bye to my parents, my two sisters and brother, and our dog, Pani (that means "Lady" in Polish). One of my family's previous pets had been named Lady. When a new puppy arrived on the scene in 1962 she was given the same name, only in another language. I can still recall the look of incredulity on the face of one of my mom's friends when we told her that Pani was sometimes locked in the bedroom when new people came over to visit. The glazed look disappeared when we explained that Pani was our German shepherd and not a human member of our household.

The walk to church took about 5 minutes. At Mass, we would have prayed for the souls of all those who had died in that heroic quest in Normandy 27 years earlier. I may have been assigned to assist the priest on the altar during that 9:00 mass. My involvement as an altar server was instrumental in turning me into a devoted baseball fan. On May 12th of 1971, our parish's altar boys went on an outing to Shea Stadium to see the Mets play the Astros. That was my initial visit to a major league game. The great Tom Seaver was the starting pitcher that day. Although my first game ended in a home team loss, I was hooked.

John Lindsay was the mayor of our city. Mr. Lindsay would play a major role in keeping the Yankees in New York by negotiating the stadium refurbishing plan and a 30-year lease with the Yankees that was signed on August 8, 1972. He would switch to the Democratic Party in August of 1971. The following year he made a failed bid for the presidential nomination and remained as mayor until Abe Beame succeeded him in 1974.

Nelson Rockefeller was the governor. The carnage at Attica, which would place a blemish on all his efforts in Albany, was just a few months away. He would move on to serve as Gerald Ford's vice president in 1974. Malcolm Wilson succeeded Rockefeller in Albany. After less than 4 months in office, Wilson would lose the gubernatorial race to Hugh Carey.

Jacob Javits and James Buckley represented New York in the Senate. Senator Javits, running off the Republican line, lost in a 1980 reelection race with Liz Holtzman and the winner, Long Island's Al D'Amato. James Buckley lost in 1976 to the legendary Pat Moynihan.

Richard Nixon was our president. The news of the day included the president's daughter's wedding at the White House scheduled for June 12th. The front page of the *New York Times* on the following Sunday, June 13th, would include coverage of the wedding, as well as the initial publication of contents from the Pentagon Papers. A little over a year would pass before we began to hear about a "third-rate burglary" at the Democratic headquarters in that apartment complex in Washington, D.C.

The Sunday *Times* cost 50 cents and the weekday version 15 cents. A slice of pizza at Sal and Tony's on Avenue A was 30 cents. A small chocolate egg cream at Andy's (now Ray's) Candy Store across from Tompkins Square Park was 20 cents. At Odessa Coffee Shop, a meat loaf (called hamburger roast on the menu) dinner with two vegetables and bread could be enjoyed for $1.15. *TV Guide* cost 15 cents. If you perused the TV listings you found the Yankees vs. Kansas City Royals scheduled at 2:00 on channel 11. The Scooter (Phil Rizzuto), Chairman of the Board (Whitey Ford), Frank Messer (in his fourth season with the Yanks), and the gold glove first baseman and new announcer Bill White (who would become president of the National League) would provide the expert commentary to those who were watching at home. Ed Sullivan was scheduled at 8:00 on channel 2. Performers on the repeat telecast included Gladys Knight, Robert Klein, and Jerry Vale. We didn't know this was to be the last really big show for Mr. Sullivan's viewers. He had been the country's Sunday night master of ceremonies for 23 years. The first of his Toast of the Town shows aired on June 20, 1948. The last original telecast was on May 30, 1971. Sullivan passed away in 1974. His show's resurgence, thanks to the proliferation of VCR's and videocassettes, would come almost 20 years after the host's death.

If the Yankee game was your choice that afternoon, you could also turn to WMCA, 570 on your AM dial. The Good Guys (fondly remembered by many New Yorkers and immortalized on the cover of the Beatles' 1967 Sgt. Pepper album) may have left the station in 1970, but the Yankees were there in 1971. One of the Good Guys, Jack Spector, stayed behind to host the sports talk show on MCA. The same announcers (with the exception of Whitey Ford) who shared their insights on TV also worked on the radio side. A few years later, in 1974, an announcer named Dom Valentino arrived in New York to do radio work exclusively for the Nets. In 1975, he joined the Yankee radio staff. His arrival marked the beginning of a trend, which saw the Yankees covered by unique teams of announcers on radio and TV. Eventually there would be separate announcer teams on radio, free TV, and cable TV. In 1971, Schaefer Beer, Datsun, ARCO, and Getty Gas were some of the sponsors.

If the Mets were your choice, you turned to channel 9 at 5:00 and watched them take on the Dodgers. Lindsay Nelson, Ralph Kiner, and Bob Murphy were the voices of the Mets. All three of those gentlemen are now enshrined in the Hall of Fame. Messrs. Nelson and Murphy were inducted as broadcasters and Mr. Kiner as a player. The Mets' radio listeners turned to WWDJ 970 AM and listened to the same trio of Hall of Famers from the TV side. The Mets' TV and radio sponsors included Rheingold beer, Manufacturers Hanover Trust, and Chrysler-Plymouth. WWDJ was a popular music station trying to carry the torch on the AM dial that had been handed down from legendary music stations like WMCA and WINS. Years later, WMCA and WWDJ would become religious programming stations. In 1972, the Mets moved to WHN 1050 AM. The station also carried games of the ABA Nets (pre-Julius Erving) and NHL Islanders. Bill Mazer was WHN's sports wizard who entertained fans with his great knowledge of all sports. Also in 1972, Jack Spector would join Mazer at WHN and be replaced at WMCA by John Sterling, who currently does Yankee radio work along with Suzyn Waldman.

On that sunny June day, I was not going to rely solely on the TV or radio to find out how the Yankees were doing. On that day, my father and I were going to the House that Ruth Built in the Bronx. It was to be my first baseball game with my father. It was the beginning of a continuing love affair with the Yankees and that beautiful ballpark. It was Bat Day. Upon entrance to the ballpark I would receive an authentic Louisville Slugger with a replica autograph from one of the Yankees. The autograph on that prize (which I still have today) was Bobby Murcer's. Mr. Murcer became my favorite Yankee. He had a great season in 1971 and would remain with the Yankees through the end of the 1974 season. Traded for Bobby Bonds at the end of the 1974 season, Murcer missed the Yankees' 1976-1978 World Series appearances. He returned during the disappointing 1979 season. I was glad to see him on the Yankee teams that participated in the 1980 American League Championship Series against the Royals and 1981's three post-season rounds against the Brewers, A's, and Dodgers. After his retirement in 1983, Bobby Murcer has remained a part of the Yankee scene and is currently a major presence during Yankee TV coverage.

To anyone reading this book, the author's goal is to put you deeply into the context of that era of the early 1970's and hopefully reawaken your own pleasant memories. The book is divided into three distinct sections: first, a description of that first game and trip to the stadium; second, the story of the season that saw the Yankees finish in fourth place in the American League's Eastern Division; and last, a look back at that time, time characterized by a number of events inside and outside of the world of baseball that marked endings or final chapters. It was my first season as a Yankee fan and the last season before the first major work stoppage in baseball that occurred prior to the 1972 season. Most of all, this book is about a special day and time for one young baseball fan and very fortunate son.

PART 1

First

As we prepared to head out to the subway on Houston Street and 2nd Avenue (right near the bocce court), my father made sure we had our transistor radio (for listening to game coverage at our seats) and that my attire was suitable for a Sunday at the ballpark. I remember both of us as fairly well dressed. No jeans or sneakers. This was to be a special day for us both, and the dress code was to reflect the day's significance. My mom looked us over, approved our fashion statements, kissed us, and gave the admonition to have a great time. Years later, when my brother-in-law and I would attend the great wrestling cards headlined by immortals like Bruno Sammartino and Jay Strongbow at Madison Square Garden, my mom would jokingly warn us to stay out of the ring. On this Sunday she didn't have to tell me to keep off the field. The thought of Yankee Stadium's hallowed ground (as Mel Allen had called it two

Junes earlier on the occasion honoring Mickey Mantle) was enough to keep me in my seat.

My father and I headed south on Avenue A toward Houston Street and then made a right toward the subway and bocce court. Sunday afternoons were very busy at the court. Many of the neighborhood's older gents would congregate there and compete. An edition of A&E's Biography series profiling the Yankee Clipper, Joe DiMaggio, contained film clips of the great DiMaggio on a bocce court in San Francisco. I don't think he ever visited or played on Houston Street and 2nd Avenue, but I am sure he would have been welcomed and might have allowed the camaraderie to penetrate his tough veneer.

After admiring some of the skills of the players on Houston Street, my father and I entered the subway train to start the journey up Manhattan's west side. At that time, the subway and bus fare was 30 cents. So our expected commutation budget for that day was $1.20. Upon arriving at the West 4th station, we heard an announcement advising of a train delay. I don't recall all the specifics, but it was clear to my father that we were going to be in for a substantial wait. Knowing how much I was looking forward to the game and seeing the time passing, my father decided that a taxi was our only option. We caught a cab fairly easily and were on our way. I appreciated my father's gesture and generosity very much then and appreciate it even more today. The meter read $20.00 by the time I saw the big blue letters on the white edifice of Yankee Stadium. That

$20.00-plus was some sacrifice for my father. Thinking about it causes me to think about another time when I was not so appreciative. In fact, I was pretty dumb and selfish. In June of 1973, on his way home from work, my father stopped off at the stadium to pick up tickets for us for a Ball Day doubleheader against the Tigers. The tickets were upper box seats in left field (section 34). When my father showed them to me I remember complaining about the location. I didn't thank him for going to pick them up after working the night shift. I sure didn't remember the thoughtfulness and generosity he had shown on that June day just two years before. It was definitely not a performance to be proud of.

Two memories really stand out about that initial entrance into the stadium. One is of my father purchasing the first souvenir for me. It was a 1971 Yankee yearbook that cost $1.00. That yearbook has survived to this day. The publication of that yearbook was well covered by the team. It was not uncommon to see Bob Fischel (Yankee PR director) come into the TV booth during a rain delay to give the fans an overview of the "information-packed volume."

To reflect for a moment on a bit of the price structure at that time, a scorecard and program cost a quarter, and the top box seat ticket in the stadium was $4.00. On the trip I had made to Shea the previous month, the Mets' 1971 yearbook was priced at 75 cents. Besides being a nice souvenir, the yearbook gave fans some hint of the team's "pecking order." The amount of text and whether a player was pictured in black and white or color indicated the player's star power. It was also helpful for a new fan like me to have pictures of the players that Bob Shepherd introduced with his perfect elocution.

The other memory most embedded in my brain is the first sight of that awesome field. The ramps in the stadium were set up in such a way that at one moment you were walking down the ramp with walls on both sides, and then, in a flash, you saw the green and brown diamond with the backdrop of the blue seats and that majestic white facade. The field was beautiful. I still get a special feeling thinking about that sight.

There was a huge scoreboard behind the right centerfield bleachers. On that scoreboard were the lineups for the game, the inning-by-inning detail, a message board in the center topped by the Yankee bat and top hat logo, and the scores from all other games. The supports for the scoreboard extended into the rear of the bleacher section. Ad space lined the base of the scoreboard and the upper portion of the back wall of the bleachers. Some of the products/companies advertised on the space during the early 70's included: Schaefer Beer, Anacin, Olins Rent-a-Car, and WMCA Radio. There were auxiliary scoreboards on the left and right centerfield walls. Those boards gave the inning-by-inning detail and the line score for the game. Before the graphics on TV became more sophisticated, the Channel 11 cameras used to focus on the auxiliary scoreboard when

Rizzuto, Messer, or White would announce the score before the half-inning commercial breaks.

In deepest centerfield, in front of the 463-foot sign were the monuments to Ruth, Gehrig, and Huggins. Plaques recognizing DiMaggio, Mantle, Ed Barrow, and commemorating the 1965 mass at the stadium celebrated by Pope Paul VI were on the outfield wall behind the monuments and flagpole. I recall one day when those monuments blocked Bobby Murcer's path to a ball hit by Harmon Killebrew. Murcer maneuvered around the monuments and got the ball back to the infield to hold Killebrew to a triple.

The Royals had taken the first 2 games of the series by scores of 6 to 2 and 11 to 7. The Yankees were looking to salvage a win to end the series and the 11 game home stand. Losing 3 straight before starting a 13 game western road trip was not an appealing thought. A crowd of 59,348 was at the Stadium on Bat Day. Before the 1973-1976 refurbishing, the stadium could hold in excess of 65,000 fans. Over 74,000 fans attended the opening game at the stadium in 1923. One of the first baseball magazines I read as a youngster was titled Baseball Extra. In the statistical section, a page listed each major league stadium's name, dimensions, and seating capacity. In 1971, if I remember correctly, Yankee Stadium was listed as seating 67,000. In 1972, the number was recorded as 65,010. Today, the capacity is in the 57,000 range. Reading that magazine and trying to let every piece of data sink in, I was confronted with one stadium's name that was confusing. The Houston Park in the NL was listed as "Domed Stadium." It took me awhile to figure out the connection to the Astrodome. Ugh!

Yankee RBI that day came from Jerry Kenney, Bobby Murcer, Roy White (the 1970's version of Old Reliable), the late Thurman Munson, and the former manager of the Expos and Giants- Felipe Alou. Stan Bahnsen pitched his third consecutive complete game, singled and scored a run. Later that season, Bahnsen would have the difficult task of pitching a Sunday matinee against Oakland's newest pitching star, Vida Blue. I recall watching that game on WPIX. One of the funniest scenes was one of the Oakland players fanning Blue with a towel after he had returned to the dugout from a trip around the bases. A lot of excitement surrounded Blue's appearance and the Yankee organization promoted it with great enthusiasm. Maybe with more enthusiasm than the Yankee players were promoted.

The Yankees' opponents that first Sunday in June, the Kansas City Royals, were in the third year of their existence and their front office was laying the foundation for the excellent teams fielded in Royals Stadium (now Kauffman Stadium) throughout the 70's and into the mid 80's. Bob Lemon was their manager. A few years later in 1978, he would lead the Yankees on an incredible journey to the World Championship, taking over the manager's job following Billy Martin's tearful resignation. The Yankees' third base coach in 1971, Dick Howser, would lead the

Royals to their only world championship in 1985. Howser managed the Yankees to 103 wins in 1980. He also was the manager of KC during the infamous 1983 Pine Tar game. The Royals had stars like Amos Otis, Cookie Rojas, and Fred Patek. Rojas and Patek were a fine double play combination. Later, Patek would team with Frank White to give the Yankees a lot of difficulties. In 1976, 1977, and 1978 the Yankees bested the Royals in the League Championship Series (best 3 out of 5). I will always remember the sight of Fred Patek alone on the bench after he hit into the series ending double play in 1977. Amos Otis, a very gifted outfielder who had toiled for the Mets at 3rd base, was the Royals' centerfielder. Dick Drago started for the Royals that day. Drago would face the Yankees many times later in the 70's as a member of the archrival Boston Red Sox.

It is interesting to note that a major theme in some of the newspaper coverage of the game was the large attendance due to the bat giveaway. Baseball's largest crowd of the season up to that point joined my father and me that day. Earlier in the week, 30,052 fans had attended one of Vida Blue's performances at the Stadium. Leonard Koppett made the point that a free bat had more drawing power than baseball's brightest new pitching star. However, 30,000 fans for a weeknight game was not a bad crowd in 1971. With this year's Yankees drawing 4,000, 000 fans, a crowd of 30,000 would be considered an aberration on the negative side.

Speaking of Mr. Koppett, he wrote a very interesting article in the Times that Sunday that offered a good amount of insight into the way fans might have perceived the Yankees of that era. It also may offer some explanation as to why the attendance and its correlation with baseball's giveaway days occupied a major position in the coverage of the Yankee victory that day.

The basic focus of the article was the 1971 Yankees' (and their fans') positions out of baseball's spotlight and in the fifth season of their commonality. Juxtaposing the Yankee successes from 1921 until 1964 with the rapid descent in their fortunes beginning in 1965, Koppett probably exacerbated Yankee fan and organizational angst. A putative lineup that included Pepitone, Richardson, Kubek, Boyer, Tresh, Murcer, White, and Munson would have forced fans' tear ducts and salivary glands into overdrive. Yet, with a few positive twists of fate, that lineup could have been performing on that 1971 Bat Day. Even more painful was the fact that the Say Hey Kid (Willie Mays), who arrived on the major league scene during the same season (1951) as the Commerce Comet (Mickey Mantle), was still playing 2 years after the Yankees retired Mantle's number. Koppett was fair in his praise of the 1971 Yankees. He did make it clear that they were not day-in or day-out excitement generators like their predecessors. Without the star power of earlier Yankee teams, free bats, balls, caps, and shirts were used to lure fans to the park. Bat Day was the most successful promotion. The following season, on June 18th, the Bat Day contest was rained out after a long delay. The young fans in attendance did get their souvenir bats. However, the Yankees scheduled a second Bat Day for an August doubleheader date against the Brewers. The move was good public relations for the team and also ensured another good crowd.

It is clear that the Yankees I saw that day were not as strong as my father's Yankees. Yet, the memories and joy "my" Yankees offered cannot be underestimated or replaced. I would have gone to the games regardless of the incentives offered. The Bombers' lineup that day began with Horace Clarke at second base. Batting second and playing third base was Jerry Kenney. Bobby Murcer in center and Roy White (the 2004-2005 Yankee first base coach) in left occupied the key third and fourth positions in the lineup. John Ellis was at first and batted fifth. The 1970 Rookie of the Year in the AL, Thurman Munson caught and batted sixth. Felipe Alou, the veteran recently acquired from the A's played right field and batted seventh. Batting eighth and playing shortstop was the future Yankee coach, manager, general manager, and head scout Gene "Stick" Michael. Batting ninth and pitching was the 1968 Rookie of the Year, Stan Bahnsen.

Those players were stars to me. They are always associated with the fondest of memories because of their roles on that June day when I was initiated into the fraternity of Yankee fans. I was already in the club of baseball fans after the May 12th trip to Shea.

The Mets team I saw that day had some truly gifted players. They were less than 2 years removed from their world title run and were still managed by the Brooklyn Dodger legend, Gil Hodges. Just to mention a few of those players evokes a sentimentality and true appreciation of their talents. Tommie Agee and Cleon Jones were exceptional hitters and outfielders. Years later, Agee worked for the same company as my sister. I made sure she knew what a special colleague she had. One day, I will have to regale her with the video highlights of the 1969 World Series and Agee's heroics. Donn Clendennon, who was such an integral contributor in 1969 and World Series MVP, was still on the team. Mr. Clendennon's signature adorned the first batting glove I used. When we played ball in Tompkins Square Park or Edison Field on 15th Street, the guys would try and emulate the mannerisms and uniform code of the major leaguers. Sweatbands and batting gloves were used by the pros, thus the kids on the Lower East Side used them.

A pitching staff with Seaver, Koosman, Gentry and Ryan would intimidate any opponent. Bud Harrelson was an All-Star shortstop and Jerry Grote, also an All-Star, excelled behind the plate. NYU alumnus, Eddie Yost coached at third, and Hall of Famer Yogi Berra coached at first. The following year, Yogi would become the manager after Gil Hodges' sudden death on Easter Sunday. That painful transition took place on the first weekend of the 1972 strike.

Entering Shea Stadium I was enthralled by the sights and sounds of the ballpark. Being there with some friends that I would remain close with to the present day added to the unique character of the day. The smell of the hot dogs, the variety of souvenirs, and the enthusiasm of the fans, Jane Jarvis at the organ, and the signs and banners displayed by the fans were a few parts of a new magical world.

Sharing New York with a team that so recently had beaten the mighty Baltimore Orioles in the World Series, added to the challenges the Yankees faced. I appreciated and respected the skills of the players in Flushing, but the Yankee players I saw that Bat Day won my allegiance. My affinity for the Yanks was also something special that I could share with my father. His allegiance to the Yankees dated back to the 1930's.

Horace Clarke was with the Yankees from 1965 until 1974. He became a full-time second baseman after Bobby Richardson's retirement in 1966. The durable Clarke was the team's leadoff hitter and did put up some impressive numbers. He led the team in stolen bases four times. For six seasons, from 1967 through 1972, he averaged over 600 at bats per season. Twice, he led the league in at bats. The AB numbers also reveal Clarke's low number of walks. The low base on balls totals exposed leadoff hitter Clarke to some criticism.

On the defensive side of the ledger, Clarke led AL second basemen in double plays two times and in assists for six consecutive seasons. Despite the fact that his career fielding statistics contain some solid figures, he is more often remembered for defensive shortcomings. One game during the 1973 season epitomizes, in my mind, Horace's situation with the Yankees. On Sunday, August 12th the Oakland A's were visiting the stadium. The world champs had spoiled the Yankees' Old Timers' festivities the previous day. The highlight of the Saturday extravaganza recognizing the stars from the Stadium's first fifty years was Mickey Mantle's home run off Whitey Ford into the left field seats. The Yankees were leading the Sunday matinee (during the pre-ESPN era, Texas, due to the intense heat, was the only venue for Sunday night games) at one point by a score of 11 to 5. The A's ended up winning 13 to 12. Unfortunately, the helmeted (Clarke wore his helmet in the field like Boomer Scott and Mr. October, Reggie Jackson years later) second baseman made a key error during the A's comeback. Four other Yankee errors were made, but Clarke's seemed to stand out then and still stands out in memory today. Ironically, Clarke and his shortstop partner, Gene "Stick" Michael worked well together and performed respectably. In 1972, they led the league in double plays. However, the Yankee pitchers like Stottlemyre, Peterson, Bahnsen, and Kline were fine sinkerballers, and they could have benefited from gold glovers behind them. In 1974, just when the Yankees were starting to benefit from the groundwork laid by Mike Burke, Lee MacPhail, and Ralph Houk (and continuing under the sound management of Gabe Paul and Bill Virdon), Clarke was traded to the Padres. Shortly thereafter, Sandy Alomar was acquired from the Angels, took over the second base job, and became a key player in that year's pennant race.

Jerry Kenney followed Clarke in the lineup and played third base. Kenney spent 4 seasons with the Yanks from 1969-1972. In his rookie year's 130 games, his fielding percentage was .975. In that same year, Hall of Famer Brooks Robinson had a .976 fielding percentage. After a sophomore year batting average of .193 in 1971, his average rebounded to .262. Following the 1972 season, Kenney was traded along with Charlie Spikes, John Ellis, and Rusty Torres to the Indians for Graig Nettles.

I recall meeting Rusty Torres outside the players' entrance after a 1972 game. As youngsters usually are, I was intrigued by how the ballplayers carried themselves and their mode of dress. Mr. Torres was wearing a pair of shoes that were red, white, and blue with stars. I thought they were really sharp. Sly Stone was pictured in a red, white, and blue outfit in the foldout section of Sly and the Family Stone's Greatest Hits album cover. Rusty Torres had the matching shoes. Boy, those guys were cool.

Bobby Murcer, who was an All-Star centerfielder and right fielder during his career, succeeded Mickey Mantle as the Yanks' resident Oklahoman star. In 1971, Murcer hit .331 with 25 HRs and 94 RBI. He finished in second place in the race for the league batting title. The great hitter for the Twins, Tony Oliva, won the title with a .337 average.

From 1971 through 1974, Murcer averaged 22 HRs and 92 RBI. Looking at those numbers, you can see why I was glad to receive a Murcer signature bat that day. It was a Louisville Slugger from Hillerich and Bradsby that had no "non-baseball" markings. In later years, the souvenir bats given out would bear the name of the company sponsoring the giveaway.

Murcer did benefit from the short right field porch in the Stadium, but I also saw him victimized by the cavernous power alley in right center. His fielding ability showed when he ran down many balls that left opposing hitters frustrated. In 1974, after he moved to right field, Murcer was the league leader in assists. In that first year in Shea Stadium (the Yanks played home games in Shea during 1974 and 1975 while the Stadium in the Bronx was being refurbished), the Yanks were quite fortunate to have an outfield of Roy White, Elliott Maddox, and Bobby Murcer. It would have been nice to have that trio remain together and share in the Yankee glories that were soon to return.

Some of the brilliant memories of my days as a Bobby Murcer fan are related to the times I would wait with my father outside the players' exit. I met Murcer and shook his hand a number of times. After an Old Timers' Day doubleheader in July of 1972, a large group of fans gathered around Murcer as he headed to the parking lot. As Bobby tried to maneuver through, he accidentally stepped on my foot. I was concerned because I thought I might have caused him to twist his ankle. Luckily, neither of us headed to the disabled list. Later that season, after a September 16th matinee against the Orioles, I ducked under the barricade and ran into the parking lot to meet Murcer. When I met up with him, I was so thrilled to meet my favorite player; I forgot to ask for his autograph. We shook hands and spoke briefly. I think I got some words out concerning the great game he had that day or what a great player he was. Many years later, my best friend who covered the Yankees for various media outlets in NY acquired the coveted autograph for me.

Roy White played left field brilliantly (and I believe that's an understatement) and batted in the cleanup spot for the Yankee teams of the early 70's. In 1971, he played the entire season without making an error. Before the modernization, left and left center fields in Yankee Stadium were huge territories. During day games and at twilight time, the sun provided a constant challenge. Despite those circumstances, Roy White put on a clinic in left field. He ran down many balls that may have eluded other fielders. During the 1974 and 1975 seasons at Shea he climbed the wall to make some home run stealing catches in the style that Dave Winfield and Ken Griffey would emulate during their tenures in leftfield with the Yanks.

Frank Messer, the Yankee announcer, gave White the nickname that Mel Allen had given the wonderful Tommy Henrich, "Old Reliable." Whether it was a clutch hit, catch, stolen base, or sac fly (White set a sac fly record in 1971),

Roy White, more often than not, came through for the Yankees. I remember listening to Bill Mazer's radio show in January of 1973 and hearing his guest, Roy White, speak about the intricacies of the game. I thought to myself that the Yankee cleanup hitter was a devoted student of the game and how lucky the Yankees were to have him on the roster. At the 1973 Old Timers' Day game against the A's, I sat with a group of my friends in the lower stand in left field. We couldn't help but watch and appreciate his skills in tracking down balls. There was one hit that White cut off in the alley, but the runner still made it to second base. I know there were many critics of White's arm strength, and that play could have given them some ammunition. But, I also know that there were many more hits stolen by number 6 than extra bases that hitters may have gotten due to his throwing arm. It seemed that every year, White's job (along with Stick Michael's) was up for grabs. Yet, on every Opening Day they were starters. As I mentioned earlier, as kids we tried to imitate the players' equipment preferences for batting gloves and sweat bands. White was the first player I recall seeing wear sweat bands on both wrists. It wasn't long before I asked my mom to make a trip to Mays' department store on Union Square or Moe's Discount Sporting Goods on Avenue A to purchase a performance-enhancing sweat band set.

As the 70's progressed and Gabe Paul acquired stronger hitters, White was able to take the 1st or 2nd spots in the lineup. He continued to thrive and contribute at the bat and in the field. In 1976, he led the league in runs scored. It was wonderful to see him celebrate the pennants and world championships of 1976, '77, and '78. It seemed that those victories were his rewards for loyal years of service to the Yankees.

John Ellis was at first base that day and batted fifth. In 1970, Ellis had won the James Dawson award given for the best rookie performance during spring training. His career began auspiciously with an inside the park homer during his first game. The aggressive playing style and displays of power at the plate from the "New London Strong Boy", gave rise to Yankee fans' hopes that they had found a performer who could hold down the position once manned by the Iron Horse, Lou Gehrig. In the Yankee yearbook of 1971, Mrs. Gehrig's best wishes for Ellis were printed. Unfortunately, Ellis did not reach those lofty heights with the Yankees. He did perform capably at first, third, and behind the plate. In 1972 he was part of the package of players sent to Cleveland in the Graig Nettles trade. He completed his career with Cleveland and Texas. Most recent press coverage of Ellis recounts his fund-raising work for cancer victims and their families.

The 1970 Rookie of the Year, Thurman Munson, played catcher that day and batted sixth. In the field, he was charged with only a single error in 1971. His sophomore year may have been a disappointment at the plate (his average dropping 50 points from his rookie year's), but for patient Yankee fans, the best was yet to come. Munson eventually was named Captain of the team; attained MVP, Gold Glove Awardee, and All-Star status; drove in 100 runs for three consecutive years; and played a vital role on three Yankee pennant winners. His passing in a 1979 plane crash was a cruel indicator of how "real" life impinges on our diversions. The Munson family members are frequent guests at Old Timers' festivities at the Stadium, and the video tribute to the Captain always evokes the cheers and tears of the crowd.

Batting 7th that day and playing right field was Felipe Alou. A .290 career hitter who had over 200 homers and 2000 hits in his career, Alou came to the Yankees in April of 1971. He was a 36-year-old veteran who helped the Yankees by playing first base, right field, and pinch-hitting. His average as a pinch hitter in 1971 was .323. In the early 60's Felipe, Matty, and Jesus Alou played in the same outfield for the Giants. All three of them eventually played in New York. Felipe and Matty contributed as members of the Yankees, and Jesus with the Mets. Late in the disappointing 1973 season, Felipe was traded to the Expos. Most recently he managed the Giants and was regarded as one of the game's fine managers.

At shortstop, hitting eighth was Gene "Stick" Michael. Along with Horace Clarke, Michael manned the middle of the Yankee infield most days from 1969 until 1973. He was well known for his penchant for the hidden-ball trick and also his scrappiness. Many fans will remember his involvement in the Fenway explosion in 1973 between

Munson and Fisk. After his retirement as a player, Michael became a Yankee coach, manager, general manager, and currently has a senior scouting position. It appears that he is enjoying his job in scouting and being away from the pressures of some of the other management positions he has held. In 1981, he was relieved of his managerial duties in September. It was tough seeing the Yankees in the Series without the man who had managed them most of the season. The current success of the Yankees is due, in no small part, to the fine work Michael did as General Manager. I hope he enjoys seeing the fruits of his labor. My father was a big Gene Michael fan. Michael's decision to slow down and take a less demanding role in the organization reminds me of how long ago it is that my father and I sat in the "old" stadium and watched the likes of Michael, Murcer, Clarke, White, and Munson.

As a fan, I've always felt players and entertainers should always be there for us and never fully retire. I know that is very selfish and also physically impossible. But, with our childhood heroes on the field or stage, we're always young, and we remain close to those with whom we shared special times. That's why Old Timers' Days or special reunion performances are always such strong attractions.

Stan Bahnsen was on the mound that day. He won the 1968 AL Rookie of the Year Award. In that year which was so full of violence and upheaval, baseball was probably a most welcome diversion. For the Yankees, 1968 - The Year of the Pitcher - saw the team finish above .500 for the first time since 1964. It was also the last year in the career of the great Mickey Mantle. As Simon & Garfunkel asked where Joe DiMaggio had gone, Yankee fans probably knew they were watching the last games of the Commerce Comet.

Bahnsen was an integral part of the Yankee pitching staff that had helped the team finish in 2nd place in 1970. Bahnsen, Stottlemyre, Peterson, Kline, and Kekich were the major starters. That group, along with bullpen help from Lindy McDaniel and Jack Aker contributed greatly to the team's 93 victories and heightened expectations for 1971 and beyond. In 1970, Bahnsen's record was 14 wins and 11 losses, 233 innings pitched, and an ERA of 3.32. As referred to earlier in this story, on Sunday, August 15th in the Bronx, Bahnsen pitched against baseball's rookie phenom, Vida Blue, in front of a crowd of over 40,000 that seemed enveloped in Vida mania. In a story befitting the entire season, the Yankee right-hander pitched capably, the Yankees battled back from a 2 run deficit, but still lost 6 to 4. Bahnsen's 1971 record (almost identical to his 1970 stats) of 242 innings pitched, 14 wins, 12 losses and an ERA of 3.35 didn't prevent the Yankees from trading him to the White Sox for Rich McKinney prior to the 1972 season. In 1972, Bahnsen won 21 games for Chicago. Unfortunately for McKinney and the Yankees, before the end of the season's second month, the new third baseman was optioned to the team's Triple A club in Syracuse. After the season, McKinney was traded to the world champs in Oakland.

My first baseball glove was a Stan Bahnsen model from Rawlings. My mom used a good stock of the Plaid Stamps she was saving and redeemed them for the glove. I am sure she wanted to use the stamps for other things, but as usual, a sacrifice was made. That glove got a lot of usage and was eventually replaced (courtesy of my brother-in-law) in May of 1975 by a Spalding Bob Gibson model. When Bahnsen is introduced at the Stadium each Old Timers' Day he is referred to as the "Bahnsen Burner." I don't recall ever hearing that nickname during his active playing days.

Managing the Yankees that day was Ralph Houk. His four-man coaching staff consisted of Jim Hegan (bullpen), Elston Howard (first base), Dick Howser (third base), and Jim Turner (pitching). Houk, known as "the Major" due to his war record, managed the Yankees from 1961 until 1963. After a term as general manager, he returned to the Yankee dugout during the 1966 season and remained until the end of 1973—the last season in the "old" Yankee Stadium. The Yankees lost the season finale on September 30, 1973 to the Tigers. My brother-in-law and I were in the crowd that day—we all received a souvenir record recounting the history of the fabled ballpark. A number of fans also took pieces of sod and seats home with them. A soft plastic version of the souvenir record was inserted in the next season's yearbook. By that time, the chairs and sod were long gone. Ralph Houk was also gone from the Yankee scene, replaced by Bill Virdon.

Houk had won the 1970 Manager of the Year award in recognition of the team's 93-win, second-place season. As was his custom, Houk credited the players and deflected the spotlight from himself. His resignation after the last game before the refurbishing of the stadium was somewhat unexpected. He still had 2 years left on his contract, and in spite of 1973's disappointments, there appeared to be reasons for optimism. Pitchers Stottlemyre, Dobson, Peterson, and McDowell appeared formidable on paper. Murcer, White, Nettles, Blomberg, Munson, and Jim Ray Hart had been pictured on one cover of the 1973 scorecard and magazine as a new "Murderers' Row." An indicant of inflation at the ballpark was the scorecard price increase to 30 cents from the previous season's quarter.

Despite the grounds for optimism, Houk left the Yankees and started the 1974 season managing and helping to rebuild the Detroit Tigers. Bullpen coach Jim Hegan went with Houk to Detroit. Pitching coach Jim Turner retired after more than half a century in baseball. The 1972 yearbook featured a photos section on Turner's 50 years in baseball. Elston Howard and Dick Howser remained with the Yankees and were in the coaching boxes when the championship flags were won in the late 70's. They also flexed their muscles (along with Yogi Berra) while separating Billy Martin and Reggie Jackson during their 1977 altercation in the Fenway dugout.

In the 1971 Old Timers' game on July 10th, Howard hit an inside-the-park home run. During my earliest days as a Yankee fan, Howard would sometimes warm up the pitcher between innings. It was fun to watch Howard work behind the plate. He would remain in the Yankee organization until his death in 1980. Howser, as mentioned earlier, would manage the Yankees and Royals, winning a world title with the Royals in 1985. A brain tumor would lead to his death in 1987.

PART 2

Fourth

There had been reason for optimism as the 1971 season approached. The Yankees had finished in second place in the A.L. East in 1970 with 93 wins. Their three main starters, Stottlemyre, Bahnsen, and Peterson, could be counted on for 15 to 20 wins and 200 innings each. Their younger starters, Steve Kline and Mike Kekich, were perceived as ready to contribute on the major league level. Jack Aker and Lindy McDaniel were a formidable bullpen team. In 1970, the bullpen had produced 49 saves. McDaniel had accounted for 29 of the save total. On offense, White, Murcer, Munson, Ellis, and Danny Cater were counted on for hefty contributions. The 1970 Manager of the Year was returning. It seemed that the rebuilding program designed by Houk, Mike Burke, and Lee MacPhail was working and would deliver in 1971. However, the Orioles of Baltimore were still the class of the A.L. East.

In some seasons, 93 victories would be enough to win the division. In 1970, the Yankees' 93 victories had not gotten them closer than 15 games behind the World Champion Orioles. Perhaps still stung by their loss to the Mets in the '69 series, Earl Weaver's team won 108 games. It is an understatement to say that the Orioles were a dominant force in baseball at that time. The 1970 season was the second of their three consecutive 100-plus win campaigns. From 1966 when the Yankees finished in the cellar and the Orioles won their first world title, until 1976 when the Yanks returned to postseason play, Baltimore finished with a less than .500 record only once, won 90 or more games eight times, won four league pennants, won the divisional title five times, and won the World Series twice (versus the Dodgers in 1966 and the Reds in 1970).

In addition to Weaver's team, the Yankees had to deal with other formidable opponents in the American League. The Tigers, managed by Billy Martin, were just three years removed from their last world championship. Their lineup included Al Kaline, Norm Cash, Willie Horton, Jim Northrup, and Bill Freehan. Mickey Lolich and Joe Coleman anchored Detroit's pitching staff. Eddie Kasko's Red Sox lineup included All-Stars Yastrzemski and Aparicio. The Indians, managed by former Giant player and dugout chief Alvin Dark (who was discharged during the season), could throw Sudden Sam McDowell at you. The Senators, managed by the Splendid Splinter (Ted Williams) and playing their final season in Washington, had slugger

Frank Howard. Out west, in addition to Dick Williams' A's and Lemon's Royals, Bill Rigney's Twins featured hitting stars Tony Oliva, Rod Carew, and Harmon Killebrew. Their pitching staff included Jim Perry, Jim Kaat, and Bert Blyleven. The Angels of California had defending American League batting champ Alex Johnson on their roster.

The 1971 season was a disappointment for the Yankees and their fans. Their spring training record was 8 and 23. A final record of 82 wins and 80 losses landed them in fourth place behind the Orioles, Tigers, and Red Sox. An even .500 finish was averted due to a victory by forfeit in the last game of the year in Washington. Hovering around the .500 mark was a yearlong phenomenon. On April 30, the Yankees' record stood at 8 wins and 10 losses. The last day of May found the team five games under the .500 mark at 21 and 26. At the end of June, the team dipped to seven games below the break-even point, with 35 wins and 42 losses. On Saturday, July 31, the team's record was 52 and 55. At the end of August as Labor Day approached, the record stood at 66 and 68.

In marked contrast to what had happened in 1970, McDaniel and Aker had their troubles in the bullpen. In 1971, the tandem of McDaniel and Aker combined for eight saves (four each). The entire save output for the team was 12. In addition to McDaniel's and Aker's work, starter Fritz Peterson earned a single save, Gary Waslewski (lost early in the year to a knee injury) had a save, and Roger Hambright preserved two victories. The bullpen's troubles contributed to the logging by the starters of 67 complete games. The team's fielding percentage was a division low of .977. Offensively, Thurman Munson's average dipped from .302 to .251. Danny Cater finished the year at .276, down 25 points from the previous season. Jake Gibbs, the Yanks' backup catcher, had batted over .300 in 1970. Gibbs' average in 1971, his retirement season, was .218. While I was preparing to write this book I was able to correspond with both Cater and Gibbs. Along with positive memories of their times with the Yankees, they recalled their frustrations with the difficulties of the 1971 season. In Philip Bashe's *Dog Days,* Roy White (who did have a solid year) states that he can barely recall that season. Five starters won 10 or more games, but no starter was more than four games over .500. There was no 20-game winner on the Yankee staff. In Baltimore, all four starters, Cuellar, Dobson, McNally, and Palmer, won 20 or more games in 1971.

New to baseball and the Yankees, I didn't let the vicissitudes of the season get to me. Apart from the special feeling of that first game, seeing Bobby Murcer start in the All-Star Game as well as the greats from both leagues, becoming familiar with Yankee history and the old-time players, watching the games with my father, beginning the hobbies of card and yearbook collecting—those are some of the things that made an 82-80 season so memorable.

Saturday, July 10, was Old Timers' Day at the stadium in 1971. It appears that the level of attention to and coverage of the Old Timers' festivities have changed over the years. Still, the day is a consistently good draw for the Yankees. Unfortunately, the Mets appear to have abandoned the Old Timers' Day concept. In 1971, both the Yankees' and Mets' days of nostalgia attracted over 43,000 fans to the ballpark. The theme of the Yankees' festivities was the 50th anniversary of the Yankees' first pennant. On July 31, at Shea, the Mets' Old Timers' festivities were focused on Bobby Thomson's fabled home run off Ralph Branca 20 years earlier. On July 11 and August 1, the *Times* offered full stories on both the regularly scheduled games and the Old Timers' games, including box scores. That type of coverage of the activities of the stars of the past does not appear in the papers today.

In the Bronx, the two-inning Old Timers' game featured two teams of former Yankees—one managed by Casey Stengel and the other managed by Stengel's successor, Ralph Houk. At Old Timers' Day the previous August, Stengel's number 37 had been retired. Stengel's lineup included Billy Martin, Phil Rizzuto, Joe DiMaggio, Tommy Henrich, Charlie Keller, Bobby Brown, Billy Johnson, Moose Skowron, and Yogi Berra. Houk's team was made up of Bobby Richardson, Hank Bauer, Mickey Mantle, Gil McDougald, Elston Howard (his inside-the-park homer was the Old Timers' only run that day), Gene Woodling, Tom Tresh, Norm Siebern, Hector Lopez, and Bill Dickey. There is not too much one can say about the amount of talent and star power of the individuals who were assembled on the Yankee Stadium field that day.

The following year, on Saturday, July 22, I attended Old Timers' Day with my father. Because of a rainout the night before, it had been necessary to schedule a doubleheader, with the Old Timers' program in between the games. We had tickets on the mezzanine level, last row, section 11. Those reserved tickets cost $3.00 each. The seats were very good, and directly behind them was a concession stand—perfect! I remember enjoying a number of hot dogs, RC colas, and French fries. I was also introduced to the pizza roll—classic ballpark fare that I can no longer find at the stadium.

The '72 Old Timers' Day theme was the honoring of five Yankee pennant winners in five different decades—in 1922, 1932, 1942, 1952, and 1962. That day the Yankees invited former Yankee heroes and some of their notable opponents. During the introductions, number 8, worn by Hall of Famers Bill Dickey and Yogi Berra (inducted into the Hall in 1972), was retired. Up to that point in time, the only other numbers the Yankees had retired were 3 (Babe Ruth), 4 (Lou Gehrig), 5 (Joe DiMaggio), 7 (Mickey Mantle), and 37 (Casey Stengel). I recall that Stan Musial made a spectacular, tumbling catch in left field that day. I also recall the thunderous ovations for Mickey Mantle and Joe DiMaggio. My father really seemed to enjoy seeing so many of the former stars, and I was glad that he was having a good time. The multiple trips to the concession stand that my father made and his willingness to wait with me outside the players' exit after a long doubleheader still evoke the deepest sense of gratitude.

An extra treat that day was seeing Nolan Ryan start the second game. It was Ryan's debut season in the American League. Before the '72 season, Ryan and a group of Met prospects, including Leroy Stanton, had been traded to the Angels for Jim Fregosi. The Yankees hit him hard in the second game of the doubleheader and won 7 to 1. In spite of the day's results, it was still evident that Ryan was a special pitcher. I can still hear the pop of the catcher's mitt receiving one of Ryan's fastballs. Ryan lasted a little more than three innings and gave up all seven Yankee runs. Future Yankee Andy Messersmith pitched four scoreless innings in relief.

In 1971, the weekend of the Old Timers' game preceded the All-Star break. That year's All-Star Game in Detroit featured an assemblage of the game's stars that included more than 10 future Hall of Famers. As with Old Timers' Days, the Mets' and Yankees' attention to the All-Star Game seems to have declined a bit over the years. In the early '70s, the Mets' yearbook regularly featured an All-Star section profiling the game and Met and non-Met participants. Also during that era, the Yankee yearbook contained a section that placed a spotlight on opposing stars from around the American League.

During the 1971 All-Star break, I was away at American Legion camp in upstate New York. I remember hearing some of the game on radio. A group of the campers also watched the game on TV. The Sunday before the midsummer classic, the Yankees played the Red Sox. That game was televised on WPIX, channel 11. The Yankee telecasts would begin and end with film clips of Yankee highlights. The Mets' telecasts also began with a film montage accompanied by an instrumental version of "Meet the Mets." The Yanks also had a theme song that was used at the start of the pre- and postgame shows hosted by Frank Messer on radio. The reason I bring up the local baseball TV coverage is that I distinctly recall thinking (erroneously) that the All-Star Game would be televised by channel 11. If Yankee players were going to be there—Murcer and Munson—then the Yankee station should cover the game. In 1971, NBC carried the game. Tony Kubek, the fine Yankee shortstop and excellent announcer, teamed up with Hall of Fame announcers Curt Gowdy and Lindsey Nelson to bring the game into viewers' homes. Kubek had been an American League All-Star in 1958, 1959, and 1961.

Before the proliferation of cable sports telecasts, the networks and the local stations offered a smorgasbord of sports programming. The New York edition of *TV Guide* for the first week of the baseball season included the schedule of Yankee and Met games to be carried on channels 9 and 11. Usually about 120 Met games and 70 to 80 Yankee games were televised during the season. Also, for the start of the baseball season, the *Daily News* Sunday magazine section contained the season's schedules for both teams.

One of my regular activities immediately before the start of the season was to take those schedules from the Sunday magazine and mark the dates of the televised games. Those schedules would then be placed on my bedroom wall for easy reference during the season.

The local TV and radio outlets were year-round sources of sports programming. WMCA had the Yankees, Jack Spector, and later on John Sterling. In 1972 when the WHA tried to compete with the NHL, the games of the new league's New York entry, the Raiders, were carried on WMCA. John Sterling and Yankee pitcher Fritz Peterson were the announcing team. WMCA also carried the games of the World Football League's New York Stars. On weekdays, Phil Rizzuto had a sports segment on the CBS network at around 6:45 p.m. At around 6:50, Stan Lomax had a segment on WOR's *Bob and Ray*. Bill Mazer held court on WHN 1050, later to be joined by Jack Spector. Jets (WOR) and Giants (WNEW) radio broadcasts featured announcers like Marty Glickman, Sam DeLuca, and Dick Lynch. The radio coverage of pro football was very important in that era before the home field TV blackout was lifted. Games of the Nets and Islanders were carried on WHN with Al Albert and Bill Mazer working the microphones. Starting in late 1972, Mazer and Lee Leonard also hosted the Sunday night sports highlight show on channel 5 called *Sports Extra*. Play-by-play for Knick and Ranger games on radio was handled by Marv Albert. On TV, channel 9 carried Knicks, Rangers, Islanders, and

Nets games. Bob Wolff and Cal Ramsey took care of the announcing on the Knick telecasts. Years later, in 1983, I saw Ramsey and Marty Glickman working together to call the game that marked the return of varsity basketball to NYU. Before the Nets moved to channel 9 with Andy Musser at the microphone, some of their Sunday night road games were carried on channel 11. The legendary Glickman teamed up with baseball Hall of Famer Bob Gibson to describe the action. ABC covered the NBA, with Chris Schenkel and Bill Russell describing the action. Channel 9 was also the home of Roller Derby (International Roller Derby League and International Skating Conference) on Saturday mornings. If you were a pro wrestling fan, the UHF stations, channels 47 and 41, carried the World Wide Wrestling Federation (WWWF) and National Wrestling Alliance (NWA). Vince McMahon and Antonino Rocca called the WWWF action. Gordon Solie was the announcer on the NWA's Florida tapings. The NWA action from LA's Olympic Auditorium aired on Wednesday evenings at 7:30. Activities in the ring were described in Spanish, but the interviews and ring announcements were in English. I can still hear the voice of the outstanding ring announcer, Jimmy Lennon, introducing stars like John Tolos, Eduard Carpentier, and Greg Valentine.

The '71 All-Star contest described by Gowdy, Kubek, and Nelson showcased a wonderful array of the most skilled baseball professionals. For the visiting National League, managed by Sparky Anderson, Willie Mays of the Giants was in center field and led off; Atlanta Braves' Hank Aaron in right field batted second; Joe Torre of the Cardinals played third base and batted third; the Pirates' Willie Stargell played left field and batted cleanup; the Giants' Willie McCovey, playing first base, batted fifth; Johnny Bench of the Reds caught and batted sixth; Glen Beckert of the Cubs, at second base, batted seventh; New York's Bud Harrelson played shortstop and batted eighth; and in the ninth spot was the starting pitcher from the Pirates, Dock Ellis. The American League starters, managed by the Orioles' Earl Weaver, had the Twins' Rod Carew in the leadoff spot; the Yanks' Bobby Murcer playing center field and batting second; Carl Yastrzemski of the Red Sox playing left field and batting third; Frank Robinson of the Orioles playing right field and batting cleanup; the Tigers' Norm Cash at first base and batting fifth; another Oriole, Brooks Robinson, playing third and hitting sixth; Bill Freehan of the Tigers catching and hitting seventh; Luis Aparicio of Boston at shortstop and hitting eighth; and Vida Blue, the sensational rookie from the Oakland A's, as the starting pitcher.

Six home runs were hit that night. Bobby Murcer (starting in place of the injured Tony Oliva) singled in his first All-Star Game plate appearance. The American League won the game 6-4 to break an eight-game losing streak (five of those eight losses by one run). The National League starter, Dock Ellis, would join the Yankees in 1976 after being acquired from the Pirates along with Willie

Randolph and Ken Brett. Blue was sent to the Yankees in 1977 during Charlie Finley's attempted fire sale. Bowie Kuhn voided that deal.

Some of the other stars who appeared in the game were Frank Howard, Amos Otis, Cookie Rojas, Mickey Lolich, Mike Cuellar, Don Wilson, Bobby Bonds, Lee May, Ron Santo, Pete Rose, Felix Millan, Lou Brock, Don Kessinger, Thurman Munson, Al Kaline, Willie Davis, and Roberto Clemente. The home run hitters that night were Bench, Frank Robinson, Aaron, Jackson, Killebrew, and Clemente. Aaron, Robinson, and Killebrew were recreating some of the magic they had displayed on the old TV show, "Home Run Derby."

Willie Mays was making his last All-Star Game appearance with the Giants. In the 1972 game in Atlanta, Mays would be wearing a Mets uniform. Acquired by the Mets in May of '72, the Say Hey Kid hit a game-winning homer in his Shea debut in the orange and blue of the team led by Yogi Berra. Mays' homer competed with the passing of TV star Dan Blocker (Hoss Cartwright on NBC's *Bonanza*) for local news coverage on that overcast Sunday.

As the summer progressed, the Yankees hovered around .500 and it became painfully clear that there would be no postseason baseball in the Bronx in '71. Like the fans of Yankee opponents from an earlier era, Bomber fans were waiting until next year. The Mets were also playing close to .500 baseball. For the second consecutive year, an 83-79 win-loss record was being forged. The only tenants at Shea in October would be the Jets. Their season didn't look very promising after Joe Namath was injured during a preseason game against the Lions. Yet, as autumn approached and a new school year began, the annual contest between the Mets and Yankees for the Mayor's Trophy drew almost 50,000 fans to Shea Stadium.

In June of 1997, New York fans were treated to a three-game regular-season series between the Yankees and Mets. Since 1958, after the departure of the Giants and Dodgers, such intracity competitions had been held solely during the exhibition season or at the annual Mayor's Trophy game. The '71 Mayor's Trophy game, held at Shea, was won by the Yankees 2 to 1. The Yankee runs were scored in the top of the ninth. The Bombers did not collect their first hit until Frank Baker singled in the top of the eighth. Jim McAndrew and Nolan Ryan held the Yankees hitless until that eighth inning. Met reliever and future physician, Ron Taylor, gave up Baker's hit and the ninth-inning runs. Yankee hurlers that day were Stan Bahnsen, Steve Kline, Alan Closter, and the late Jim Hardin.

Even though the game did not count in the standings, fans did pay attention to the game and its outcome. There was a sense that the victor earned some type of "bragging rights." The contest and its meaning could be compared to the annual preseason football matchup of the Jets and Giants. I recall having my GE transistor radio in hand to listen to the Trophy game while my mom and I traveled by bus to JFK airport, formerly known as Idlewild, to meet my sister, who was returning from a vacation. I am sure the more "sophisticated" fans were a little more relaxed about the September 9 contest at Shea than my friends and I were.

The game lasted slightly over two hours. The Yankees' lack of a hit until the eighth and the Mets' lone score, coming in the first inning, contributed to the quick pace. For the Yankees that day, Jerry Kenney was at third base; Thurman Munson and John Ellis split the catching duties; Ellis and Danny Cater shared first base responsibilities; Ron Swoboda was in center field; Roy White and Jim Lyttle covered left field; Rusty Torres and Lyttle shared right field; Horace Clarke and Ron Hansen patrolled second base; and Frank Baker played shortstop.

The Mets' participants included Ted Martinez at shortstop, Wayne Garrett and former Brooklyn Dodger Bob Aspromonte at third base, Dave Marshall in left field, Ed Kranepool and Donn Clendennon at first base, Art Shamsky in right field, Ken Singleton in center field, Duffy Dyer and Jerry Grote catching, and Tim Foli in the middle of the diamond at second base.

Entering the game, both teams were near the .500 mark. The Yanks' record was 71 and 72; the Mets' was 72 and 69. Both teams were in fourth place in their divisions. The Yanks trailed Baltimore by 18 1/2 games. The Mets were 13 1/2 games behind Danny Murtaugh's Pirates. The Mayor's Trophy game added some spark to the final month of a season that for many fans may have lost its luster earlier that summer.

Three weeks later on Thursday, September 30, the Yankees' final game of the season took place in Washington's Robert F. Kennedy Stadium. The game marked the end of baseball in the nation's capital. A small but vocal crowd of 14,460 fans congregated to cheer for the Senators, recognize the passing of baseball from the Washington scene, and vent their anger at owner Bob Short. Banners on display included barbs such as "We were Short-changed." The mundane message "So long Short" was modified to read "So long $hort." Just about a decade earlier, Calvin Griffith had packed up and moved his Senators to Minnesota, renaming them the Twins. Don Mincher, who was on the Senators' roster in '71 and who would pinch-hit in the '71 finale, was also a part of the previous Senator team that had transferred to Minnesota. After the Griffith move, another team was quickly created for D.C. It would be more than 30 years after Short's Senators left, though, before Major League Baseball would return to D.C. After the Yankee-Senator finale, the Redskins would become the primary tenant in the stadium that had recently been named after the former attorney general and U.S. senator from New York, murdered in June of 1968 after winning the Democratic primary in California.

On that last day of September I was not feeling well and had missed a day of school. One thing I remember about my hours of TV viewing that day was a talk show telecast over channel 4. The show, originating in Chicago, was hosted by Phil Donahue. The rapport that the host had with the audience and guests was evident. The format of the show differed from that of the other popular talk shows of the era. Mike Douglas hosted a syndicated daytime show. David Frost held court during the prime-time hours on New York's Metromedia TV channel 5. Late-night network TV offered Carson, Cavett, and Griffin. Years later, one could find cuts from the Douglas and Cavett shows on VH-1. A syndicated series showcasing classic skits and routines from the *Tonight Show* introduced the great Johnny Carson to new viewing generations.

The Yankee season finale was not carried by channel 11. I planned to avail myself of the coverage provided by the Yankee broadcast trio over WMCA 570 AM. A special guest in the radio booth that night was Yankee President Mike Burke.

Frank Messer's pregame show featured a conversation with Yankee starter, Mike Kekich. Bill White and Frank Messer led off the broadcast and described the anti-Bob Short sentiment that was pervading the stadium. A commercial for Schaeffer beer intervened between the broadcasters' opening remarks and the introduction of the starting lineups. Bobby Murcer batted in the leadoff spot that night. Manager Houk was taking every step to help Murcer get the hits needed to surpass the league batting leader from the Twins, Tony Oliva. The first spot in the order could afford Murcer more at-bats than his customary third spot. Murcer's task was Herculean. In order to surpass Oliva (.337 average), the Yankee center fielder (.331 average) needed six hits in six at-bats.

At second base and batting second was Horace Clarke. Recently called up from the minor leagues, Rusty Torres played right field and hit third. Roy White, looking to play one more errorless game in left field to maintain his perfect fielding average, was in the cleanup spot. John Ellis, batting fifth, was the first baseman. Thurman Munson caught and hit sixth. Third baseman Ron Hansen and shortstop Frank Baker covered the left side of the infield and occupied the seventh and eighth spots in the batting order. Mike Kekich, with a 10-9 win-loss record, was the starting pitcher and ninth hitter.

The Senators' lineup for this farewell game started with Elliott Maddox, the center fielder. Shortstop Toby Harrah batted second. Both Maddox and Harrah would eventually spend time in Yankee uniforms. Maddox became the team's starting center fielder after his arrival in 1974. Toby Harrah would log some time in Yogi Berra's 1984 infield. Batting third and playing first base was fan favorite and power hitter Frank Howard. The catcher, Dick Billings, batted fourth. Jeff Burroughs played left field and was the fifth-place hitter. Third baseman, Dave Nelson, followed Burroughs to the plate. The final third of the order consisted of the right fielder, Del Unser (the lone left-handed hitter in the Senators' starting nine), second baseman Tom Ragland, and starting pitcher Dick Bosman. The right-hander was making his 35th start and entered the game with a 12-16 win-loss record. Bosman later served as the Texas Rangers' pitching coach.

After their first turn at bat, the Yankees had two runs on the board. Those runs came courtesy of a Rusty Torres home run to right and an RBI single off the bat of John Ellis. Roy White scored from second on the first baseman's hit following his own double to left. The bottom half of the first, although it ended with the Yanks' two-run advantage, gave some indication of the team's season-long defensive challenges. Maddox led off with a grounder to short. The center fielder was out at first despite a high throw by Baker. Harrah, the next hitter, beat out an infield hit to shortstop. During the game, the Yankees would be charged with five errors. E6 (an error by the shortstop) was flashed on the scoreboard three times. One error each was charged to pitcher Aker, third baseman Hansen, and late-inning shortstop Michael. Two were charged to Baker. In Bashe's *Dog Days,* Baker recounts his problems that started with illness in spring training and just seemed to plague him all year.

The Yankees doubled their run output with a two-run second inning. After one out, Baker drew a base on balls. Kekich then sacrificed him to second. Murcer, in his second turn at bat, hit a two-run homer to right center field. His fly out to left to open the game had erased his chances for the hitting title, but he was still in there hacking. The homer lengthened Murcer's consecutive-game hitting streak to 15 games.

In the bottom of the second frame, the Senators scored an unearned run. The inning ended with Bosman grounding into a Baker-to-Clarke-to-Ellis double play. Hansen, Clarke, and Ellis had joined forces to end the Senators' first inning. Baker got into the act in this second inning.

As the broadcast progressed, Yankee President Mike Burke entered the booth and added his comments and observations. Throughout his conversation with the Yankee announcers, Burke showed his support and empathy for the players in his employ. He was quite impressed with the newcomer in right field, the switch-hitting Torres. Also singled out for special praise was Roy White. The left fielder had handled over 300 chances flawlessly throughout the season, and Burke made sure to commend the effort. In the top of the fifth, Burke and Bill White were discussing the next season and players who might be making future contributions. Players mentioned included the Triple A Syracuse middle infield tandem of Fred Frazier and Mario Guerrero, as well as current Yankee infielder Jerry Kenney. Burke's earlier praise of White seemed prophetic as number 6 hit the Yanks' third homer of the night in New York's half of the fifth inning.

As John Ellis came to bat, Burke thought back to the first baseman's inaugural game with the Bombers, in which he had hit an inside-the-park home run and Stan Bahnsen had pitched a two-hit shutout. Earlier in the game, Messer and White had discussed Ellis' efforts to get his batting average over the .240 mark for the season. Some of his season's difficulties were attributed to the disruption caused by his military reserve duties. Before conscription ended during the Nixon administration, it was not uncommon for players to miss parts of seasons or entire seasons to fulfill their military obligations. In the statistical section of the yearbook, certain players' entries read "In Military Service" instead of providing the normal figures for HR, RBI, Avg., Wins, Losses, or ERA. Bobby Murcer's 1967 and 1968 seasons were spent in the service.

Burke's concern for and interest in the players were evidenced by his mention of the illness of Thurman Munson's mother. It was surmised that the concerns for his mom might have contributed to some of Munson's difficulties at the plate in his sophomore year. As the fifth inning ended with Toby Harrah hitting into a 6-6-3 Baker-to-Ellis double play, the Yankees led 5 to 1. Between the fifth and sixth innings, Bill White read a commercial from ARCO offering packages of a dozen 8-by-10 player photos. The "picture paks" cost $1.00 and were available for the Yankees, Red Sox, Phillies, and Pirates. At the stadium, one could purchase a similar souvenir. I still have the pak that my father purchased for me. The photos, which came in a clear plastic envelope, were of Alou, Blomberg, Murcer, Peterson, Swoboda, and White.

In the top of the sixth, Murcer walked following a Baker strikeout and Kekich groundout. Murcer's chances of catching Oliva for the batting crown having evaporated, Burke and White waxed on about what might have been. They mentioned that Murcer's average would have been enough to win the American League crown in 1968 (when Yaz hit .301 for the Red Sox) or 1970 (when California's Johnson won the batting championship with a .329 mark). After his base on balls, Murcer stayed at first as Clarke popped out to the left side. In the last half of the sixth, Washington came back to tie the score against Kekich and Jack Aker. During the home team's rally, White and Burke lamented the bullpen's 1971 troubles. Hope was expressed for the relief corps to return to form in '72 and to join forces with the strong starting staff that included the young Kekich and Steve Kline.

The Scooter, Phil Rizzuto, arrived in the booth as the seventh inning commenced. The all-time Yankee shortstop joined Burke in awarding Bill White the Rookie of the Year honors. White also was the recipient of some dieting advice to follow over the winter, courtesy of the Hall of Fame shortstop who had made his major league debut in Washington in 1941. With the score still tied at 5, the seventh inning ended and Burke prepared to exit the booth. Still behind the microphone in the top of the eighth, Burke mentioned how glad he was to be able to meet former Yankee and Senator manager Bucky Harris, who was attending the game. Rizzuto, in turn, mentioned his positive experiences as a player for Harris in 1947 and 1948. In their turn at bat, the Yanks got one man to first as Munson bunted for a single. Hansen hit into a 6-4-3 double play. Then Stick Michael, hitting for Baker, lined out to third. Before the Senators took their eighth-inning turn at bat, Burke thanked Rizzuto, Messer, and White for their efforts in 1971 and signed off.

In the bottom of the eighth, the left side of the Yankee infield was charged with two errors. The Senators scored twice. RBI came from future Mets hitting coach Tom McCraw and future Yankee (as well as future Oriole and Met) Elliott Maddox.

Several years later, on Friday night, June 13, 1975, as part of the Con Ed Kids program, a group of my friends and I attended a Yankee-White Sox game at Shea Stadium. During that game, Maddox seriously injured his knee. He was never the same player after that. In '74 he had hit over .300 and was a fine addition to the Yankee outfield. In '75, he was above .300 at the time of the injury. The Yanks had finished second in 1974 and were capable of winning the division in '75 under Bill Virdon. Catfish Hunter and Bobby Bonds had been added to the roster after the 1974 season. Unfortunately, in 1975, the injury bug struck the Yankees. Bonds ran into a wall in Chicago and hurt his knee; Lou Piniella had inner ear troubles all year; Roy White lost some playing time (a very rare occurrence in a career marked by durability); Blomberg's chronic shoulder troubles robbed him of his quick swing; and Maddox went down and didn't return until 1976, encumbered by a bulky knee brace.

In the eighth inning of the '71 D.C. finale, the fans began to run on the field and disrupted the game. As the ninth inning began, with the home team leading 7 to 5, left-hander Joe Grzenda took the ball with the goal of forcing the final three outs from Felipe Alou, Bobby Murcer, and Horace Clarke. Alou grounded to short and Murcer bounced one to the pitcher. Horace Clarke never got his turn at bat that inning. A surge of fans onto the field resulted in a 9 to 0 forfeit victory for the Yanks.

Baseball for the '71 Yankees was over. The Senators, the last American League team to represent Washington, D.C., finished with 63 wins and 96 losses. The Yankees finished with 82 victories and 80 losses. Due to the forfeit on the final day, the Yankee pitching staff was credited with only 81 regular-season wins. There was no Yankee winning pitcher in the finale because the Yanks were trailing at the time the fans took over the field and the game. After about 2 3/4 hours of broadcast time, Bill White and Frank Messer acknowledged their colleagues in the Yankee organization and on the broadcast staff. WMCA's first spring training game was a little more than five months away.

PART 3

Last

As I looked out on a partially snow-covered 6th Street, an advertisement came on over WMCA. Before the nightly sports call-in program was to return, listeners were enticed by the thought of the first Yankee preseason broadcast. The Yankee theme song and Frank Messer's voice made the radio spot complete. Just about a month later, on Good Friday, the dreaded announcement came. The owners and players had reached an impasse and a work stoppage had been approved by the players. Opening Day, scheduled for Thursday, April 6, 1972, in the Bronx, was in grave jeopardy. As I watched the Knicks-Bullets playoff game that evening on WOR channel 9, I couldn't suppress the great sadness I felt about the turn of events in baseball. I didn't know it at the time, but 1971 was to have been my last season as a fan of a sport uninterrupted by labor and management disputes.

During the spring of 1972, a sports fan in New York had many diversionary options. The Knicks were on their way to another championship series versus the Los Angeles Lakers. The Rangers would make it to the Stanley Cup final round against the Boston Bruins led by Bobby Orr and Phil Esposito. In 1972, the NHL had a national TV contract with CBS. The "Tiffany Network" cameras brought the sights and sounds of the final series into our living rooms. Both tenants of Madison Square Garden lost in the 1972 final rounds. The Rangers would work and wait until 1994 for their next Stanley Cup victory. The Knicks would come back to beat the Lakers in the 1973 NBA finals. That '73 series was to be the last hurrah for that awesome team led by Reed, Frazier, Bradley, DeBuscherre, Monroe, and Holtzman. The championship round of 1973 was the last televised by ABC. CBS would get the NBA contract starting with the 1973-74 season. CBS stopped NHL coverage after the Bruins-Rangers '72 final. NBC with Tim Ryan, Ted Lindsay, and "Peter Puck" started covering the NHL in the 1972-73 season. CBS covered the new WHA in its inaugural 1972-73 year.

Out in Nassau County on Long Island, the ABA Nets, coached by Lou Carnesseca and featuring Rick Barry, John Roche, Tom Washington, and Bill Melchionni (injured for the playoffs), made it to the ABA finals against the Indiana Pacers of Mel Daniels, Roger Brown, and Billy Keller. CBS, with Don Criqui at the microphone, covered the sixth and final game of the championship series from the brand-new Nassau Coliseum. The Pacers won that game as a flu-weakened Rick Barry couldn't push his team over the top in his final game as a Net. After the season, Barry would leave his spot on the Nets roster and his job as a local sportscaster, and return to the NBA's Golden State Warriors.

As I mentioned earlier, the '71 season was my last baseball season undisturbed by the cacophony and animosity of protracted labor-management negotiations and work stoppages. Looking back, I realize that the year 1971 included several events that marked the endings of eras in the world beyond baseball.

In June of that year, the Fillmore East on Manhattan's 2nd Avenue closed its doors. On June 6, the late Frank Zappa was on the bill. Around 1970, Zappa and his Mothers of Invention released a double album on Verve titled *Freak Out*. The album had some interesting cuts and some cover art that was a bit creepy.

The Doors were still enjoying high levels of success and popularity four years after the release of "Light My Fire." Early in the summer of 1971, Jim Morrison, their lead singer, died in Paris. Fans were stunned, the group tried to carry on before eventually disbanding, and the Morrison legend continued to grow. In May of 1971, George Harrison came into Madison Square Garden for the Concert for Bangladesh. The event was heavily covered by the New York media. Geraldo Rivera, working for New York's channel 7 at the time, delivered the story on

Eyewitness News. Rumors were circulating of a potential reunion of the four Beatles. That reunion did not occur at the concert, and the end of an era for Beatle fans hit home when the 1970 breakup was reconfirmed.

On TV, as mentioned earlier, Ed Sullivan's Sunday night run ended after almost 23 years. Johnny Carson was basing his *Tonight Show* in New York City for the last full year. In 1972, the show would switch to Burbank and remain there until Carson's retirement in 1992. The 1971-72 season would be the last in which the three leading actors in NBC's *Bonanza* (Lorne Greene, Dan Blocker, and Michael Landon) would work together. Blocker's death in May of 1972 would prematurely end the show and alter the Sunday night viewing habits of many. The show had been an important part of NBC's prime-time lineup since the presidency of Eisenhower. In the early 1960s, Vaughan Meader had enjoyed great success on stage and in the recording studio with his impersonation of President Kennedy. One of his album cuts involved a mock presidential press conference that included a query about a weekly TV show featuring the First Lady. Meader, playing the role of JFK, responded that the show's slot, opposite *Bonanza*, prevented him from viewing his wife's program.

America's TV viewing habits were changing or, more accurately, were being forced to change. The sitcoms and variety shows that had been prime-time staples and that offered escape during the turbulent Vietnam era left the air in rapid fashion. Andy Griffith left his law enforcement position in Mayberry in 1968. Jackie Gleason's and Red Skelton's shows ended in 1970 and 1971, respectively. Also in '71, Andy Williams ended production of his Saturday night NBC program. Between 1970 and 1972, ABC's *Bewitched* and CBS's *My Three Sons* and *The Beverly Hillbillies* left the prime-time schedule.

As American ground troops spent their last full year in Vietnam (the last U.S. ground troops left in August of 1972), the folks back home heard of My Lai, Vietnamization of the war, and the Pentagon Papers. Very soon, "Watergate" would enter the lexicon. World and national events were communicated to us on CBS by Walter Cronkite, with Eric Severeid offering his commentary; on NBC by John Chancellor and commentator David Brinkley; and on ABC by Frank Reynolds and Howard K. Smith (who also had a commentary role). Local events in the New York area were reported by Bill Beutel and Roger Grimsby on channel 7, Jim Jensen on channel 2, and Jim Hartz on channel 4. Buffeted by the news of the day from Saigon and Washington, D.C., the American TV viewing public would no longer enjoy the calming influences of the Stephens, Douglas, and Clampett families.

On the baseball field, the 1971 World Series between the Orioles and Pirates was the last Fall Classic for Roberto Clemente. His .414 average helped Pittsburgh triumph in seven games. In 1972, Clemente collected his 3,000th hit off the Mets' Jon Matlack. The Pirates won the N.L. East for the third consecutive season, but lost to the Reds in the N.L. Championship series. Clemente died in a plane crash on December 31, 1972, en route to earthquake-ravaged Nicaragua. That 1971 season was also the last for Gil Hodges. In 1953, a borough prayed for him during a tough batting slump. After his death on Easter Sunday in 1972, the world of baseball mourned his loss and prayed for his family. He had been stricken by a first heart attack during a game in Atlanta on September 24, 1968. The fatal attack occurred on April 2, 1972, as Hodges and three of his coaches (Eddie Yost, Rube Walker, and Joe Pignatano) returned to their hotel after 27 holes of golf. Less than three years earlier, Hodges had managed the Miracle Mets to a five-game World Series win over the Orioles. In four seasons at the helm, his Mets teams finished ninth, first, and third (the latter twice, in 1970 and 1971). The news of his passing relegated thoughts of the strike to the bench. To this day, Met Hall of Famer Tom Seaver mentions the passing of Hodges as the beginning of a long decline for the Mets organization.

Prior to the 1971-72 season, the Giants announced that they were leaving Yankee Stadium and would eventually play in a new stadium in New Jersey. As a follow-up to the Giants' announcement, channel 2 in New York produced a documentary entitled "The Giant Step." The program outlined some of the reasons for and implications of the move. The economics of the move were not that important to a nine-year-old viewer. They were probably more significant to the New York officials who were negotiating to keep the Bombers in the Bronx.

The top New York official, John Lindsay, was monitoring the negotiations and was also preparing for a 1972 quest for the Democratic presidential nomination. Lindsay had switched his party affiliation and was looking for a chance to challenge President Nixon in November of 1972. Nixon and Agnew won by a landslide over McGovern and Shriver in the '72 election. The impact of Watergate had not yet become overwhelming. However, distrust of government officials and cynicism about their motives would begin to grip our country's soul as more Americans became aware of the sordid affair that began in June of 1972.

On September 11, 1971, an old nemesis of the United States, Nikita Khrushchev, passed away. Just nine years earlier he had been leader of the U.S.S.R. as the Cuban missile crisis brought the world to the brink of nuclear war. Who knew that 30 years later, September 11 would be seared into the world's memory for vastly different reasons.

All of the events that I've discussed throughout this narrative may not be equally significant in the history of our country. To me, the closing of Pallisades Amusement Park or the departure of the Giants from Yankee Stadium were more understandable and had more impact than the complications of President Nixon's wage and price controls or the significance of Khrushchev's passing. Also, the happenings in the world of sports and entertainment helped to forge lasting bonds with my father and with my original circle of friends. Those bonds are still strong today, 30 years after my graduation from grammar school and my father's death.

A Fan's Quest

As I prepared to record my thoughts and recollections for public consumption, I attempted to contact a number of Yankee announcers, coaches, and players from the 1971 season. In some cases, my address file was not current. Some of the individuals I did reach did not respond. Ralph Houk, Jim Turner, and Roy White were kind enough to send back responses, but their schedules did not allow them to talk to me. Bobby Murcer did respond with a note stating that contractual obligations prohibited him from contributing to the book. Horace Clarke, Jake Gibbs, Danny Cater, and Steve Kline did respond and shared some of their remembrances with me. Their memories of that era with the Yanks were quite clear. I appreciate the courtesy and time of those former Yankees.

It was thrilling to have a chance to speak to Gibbs and Kline. The written responses from Cater and Clarke were very thorough. A copy of my interview questions is included in the appendix. The questions were designed to give me some indication of how the men who were in the arena in 1971 felt about those days and all their days with the Yanks.

The respondents expressed their appreciation of the unique aura that accompanied playing for the Yankees in that grand stadium. Danny Cater's most pleasant memory of playing in Yankee Stadium was "going out to play first base for the first time and thinking I'm standing where Lou Gehrig played." Horace Clarke stated, "When I was promoted from the Triple A level to the big leagues I was in awe." Jake Gibbs mentioned the chills he got when he played on the diamond in the Bronx. Steve Kline mentioned the aura of the place and its history and lore. I also inquired about recollections of Old Timers' Days. The respondents mentioned encounters from their playing days with stars like DiMaggio, Mantle, Henrich, Stengel, Reynolds, and Dugan. Now that they participate in the Old Timers' festivities, the former players mentioned the fun that goes with seeing their former mates, reminiscing, and playing in the two- or three-inning game that caps off the day.

The recollections and feelings of the '71 players who answered my queries were, in some respects, similar to my own. They expressed an appreciation of the Yankee tradition that existed up to that time, a respect for their Yankee teammates and their many skilled opponents, and an affection that was not overly maudlin. Okay, maybe that's where the respondents and I differ. I admit that my feelings about that era are a bit maudlin, and maybe just slightly romanticized.

Final Thoughts

One may ask why someone would write down memories of baseball, sports, and TV shows when there is so much "more important" stuff going on in our world. I won't deny the validity of such an inquiry. I would respond that I recorded the memories because they're pleasant, and that the act of writing them down was very pleasant. I also wanted to share them with others because I believe there are many people who fondly recall the era I've focused on. Despite what Scarlett O'Hara's father told her about the permanence of the soil of Tara, memories are the only things that last. Memories help us to get through the ups and downs of our daily lives. They sustain us when friends and loved ones leave us. The people who contribute to those good memories deserve our thanks.

Over the last few years, we've lost people like Tommie Agee, Donn Clendennon, Red Holzman, and Dave DeBuscherre. Mel Stottlemyre and Gene Michael, who contributed so much to the Yankee resurgence in the 1990s, have moved on or had their roles greatly reduced. Bobby Murcer is currently going through treatments after removal of a brain tumor. I wanted to put my appreciation to those people in writing before any more time passes.

I also want to make it clear that in focusing on the 1971 Yankees and the times of my youth, I am not trying to disparage the players or the game of today. I still love baseball and the Yankees. The recent Showalter and Torre eras in Yankee history and the players who have contributed to such great achievements have really spoiled us.

Is my view of the game different today? Of course it is. I am approaching my 45th birthday. Two of the three men who introduced me to the world of sports, my father and uncle, died in 1975. After they died, my brother-in-law made sure I stayed immersed in the sports world. Thank God, I still have my mom, wonderful siblings, family, friends, and a precious wife and daughter. So baseball occupies a smaller part of my life in 2007.

Would I want to be transported back to relive the days I've written about here? I don't think so. They were priceless the first time around. Am I glad I lived during those times and formed my attachment to the Yankees and baseball back then? You bet!

Sources

In addition to my own personal recollections and memorabilia collection, a number of external information sources were consulted. The *Newark Star-Ledger* and *New York Times* were the periodical sources. The *Sport Americana Baseball Address List* (number 8) by R.J. Smalling, published by Edgewater Book Company, was very useful. Two fine books that offer information on the Yankees of the '60s and '70s are Philip Bashe's *Dog Days: The New York Yankees' Fall from Grace and Return to Glory, 1964-1976*, published by Random House; and *They Kept Me Loyal to the Yankees* by Victor Debs, published by Rutledge Hill Press. In the TV history area I consulted the third edition of *The Complete Directory to Prime Time TV Shows 1946-Present* by Tim Brooks and Earle Marsh, published by Ballantine Books. Media sources included ESPN's Classic Sports Network; audiotapes from the Miley Collection of Evansville, Indiana; and Doak Ewing's Rare Sportsfilms of Naperville, Illinois.

Appendix—Research Questions to be sent to members of 1971 Yankees

First of all, thank you for agreeing to help with my book research. I have put together a group of questions that I think will help me as I map out the themes I want to cover in the book. Basically, I am hoping that your answers to the questions will offer a view of your memories and feelings about your time with the Yankees. I have included copies of Yankee yearbook pages and statistics that may help refresh your memory. As I promised in my original letter to you, I do not plan to write anything disparaging about baseball or the players (past and present) who make the game so special. In the book I want to try and convey a time (my first season as a baseball fan) that is the source of very special memories. Thanks for your help.

On the following pages, you will find the questions listed and space to write in your replies. If you need more space to write, feel free to continue on the back of the pages. Also, there are some blank pages on which you can continue your answers or offer any additional comments.

Q.1   Please share your most pleasant memory of playing in the old Yankee Stadium.

Q2.   Please share with me your most pleasant memory of your career with the Yankees.

Q3.   Looking back on your Yankee career, what was your biggest disappointment?

Q4. What was the most difficult part of your job as a baseball player?

Q5. What was the easiest (if there was one) part of your job as a baseball player?

Q6. How do you keep in touch with baseball today?

Q7. Do you have any special memories of the 1971 season? If yes, please discuss them.

Q8. What was it like playing in New York City during your career?

Q9. What are your memories of the "Old Timers' Day" gatherings at Yankee Stadium? What is your most special memory of those Old Timers' Days?

Q.10 Who were the best hitters you played with and against?

Q.11 Who were the best pitchers you played with and against?

Q.12 What are your memories of the fans and media during your time with the Yankees?

Q.13 What advice (if any) do you have for a youngster pursuing a baseball career?

IMAGES
All images courtesy of the author.
Photography by Harisch Studios of Ridgewood, NY.

78 FIRST, FOURTH AND LAST

'23 Scorecard Cover: Replica of the 1923 Stadium Opening Day Scorecard that was given out to fans attending the Stadium Opener on April 15, 1973

All Images Courtesy Of The Author

'71 Cover: Cover of the first souvenir my father purchased for me at the Stadium on Bat Day, June 6, 1971

Photography By Harisch Studios

80 FIRST, FOURTH AND LAST

'71 Schedule: Schedule and ticket info page from the 1971 Yearbook. Look at those prices and the number of scheduled doubleheaders.

All Images Courtesy Of The Author

'72 OT: Souvenir program that was distributed on Old Timers' Day of 1972 honoring pennant winners of 1922, 1932, 1942, 1952, 1962.

Photography By Harisch Studios

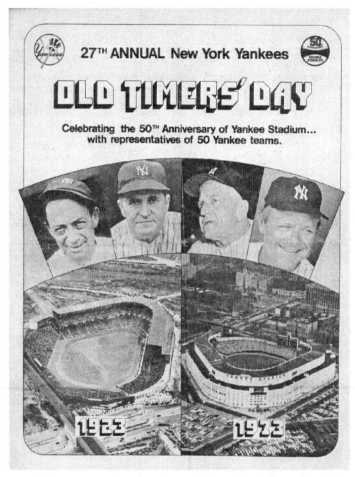

'73 OT: Souvenir program that was distributed on Old Timers' Day of 1973 celebrating 50 years of Yankee Stadium

All Images Courtesy Of The Author

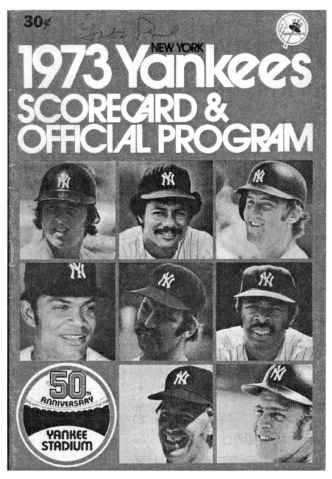

'73 Scorecard Cover: Scorecard purchased on April 15, 1973. Gabe Paul autograph is visible at the top.

Photography By Harisch Studios

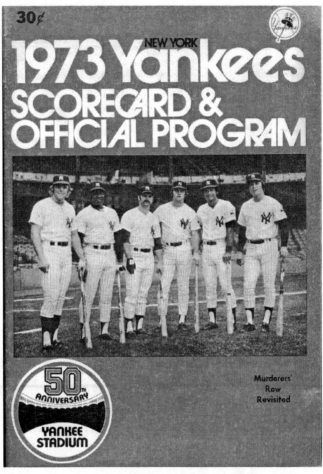

'73 Scorecard Cover: Purchased on Bat Day of 1973 with cover depicting the new Murderers' Row.

All Images Courtesy Of The Author

Fiftieth Anniversary of Yankee Stadium phonograph record that was inserted in the 1974 Yearbook.

Photography By Harisch Studios

Team Poster that was the centerfold of the 1972 Yearbook.

All Images Courtesy Of The Author

Scorecard: Yankee Lineup in scorecard from Bat Day 1972 (June 18th) against Texas that was rained out.

Photography By Harisch Studios

ISBN 1425111319